At Home in the RAIN FOREST

by Diane Willow
Illustrated by Laura Jacques

Charlesbridge

Published by Charlesbridge Publishing, 85 Main Street,
Watertown, MA 02172 • (617) 926-0329

Printed in the United States of America
(sc) 10 9 8 7 6 5 4 3
(hc) 10 9 8 7 6 5 4 3 2
(lb) 10 9 8 7 6 5 4 3 2 1

Printed on Recycled Paper.

Library of Congress Cataloging-in-Publication Data
Willow, Diane.
  At home in the rain forest / by Diane Willow; Laura Jacques,
illustrator.
    p.   cm.
  Summary: From the tops of the tropical trees to the forest
floor, this book shows the interrelationships of plants and
animals which thrive at each level of an Amazonian rain forest.
  ISBN 0-88106-688-5 (library reinforced)
  ISBN 0-88106-485-8 (trade hardcover)
  ISBN 0-88106-484-X (softcover)
  1. Rain forests–Juvenile literature.   2. English language–
Juvenile literature. [1. Rain forests. 2. Amazon River
region.] I. Jacques, Laura, ill. II. Title.   91-70014
574.5 — dc20   CIP
                                                        AC

Raindrops roll off the tips of thick, waxy leaves, making a drip, drip, dripping sound. When the cool rain stops falling, a breeze shakes the treetops. In the highest branches of the tropical trees, billions of bright green leaves catch the light of the returning sun. From above, the leaves look like one huge green ocean. Like an ocean, the rain forest shelters many creatures.

Brazil nut tree

kapok tree

fig tree

cecropia tree

At dawn, the bats finish drinking the nectar from the night-blooming kapok flowers. They swoop back to their home in a hollow tree. There they will sleep all through the day.

Perched in the kapok tree is a harpy eagle — the largest eagle in the world. Even though the eagle is three and one half feet tall, none of the creatures below notices it. The eagle is watching them wake up as a new day dawns in the Amazonian rain forest.

harpy eagle

South American long-tongued bat nectar eating bat

aechmea chantinii

kapok pod & flower

Suddenly, the hungry harpy eagle flies from its perch. Diving full speed into the leafy canopy, the enormous bird twists and turns between the large branches.

A startled troop of howler monkeys leaps quickly away. Swinging from tree to tree on looping liana vines, all but one escape.

cattleya orchid

red howler

philodendron

liana vines

The monkeys gather in the branches of a cecropia tree. The male howler monkeys announce their new territory with a trumpeting "aghooooowagh." Their deafening roars can be heard over a mile away.

The forest is full of other sounds. A big woodpecker pecks "rap-ta-ta-tap," looking for ants and beetle larvae beneath the bark of a broken balsa wood tree. Cicadas, the world's loudest insects, rub their front wings together making their "eeeee—ooooh, eeeee—oooh" siren sound.

A passionflower butterfly is the only silent one. It drifts quietly by a heavy pod of ripening Brazil nuts.

cicada

Brazil nut pod

passion-flower butterfly

The passionflower butterfly heads toward a vanilla bean. The bean is the seed pod of a vanilla orchid that grows high up on a branch. The scent of vanilla drifts from the ripened vanilla bean, sweetening the moist forest air.

The passionflower butterfly stays out of reach of a pygmy marmoset. This marmoset is so small it could curl up in the palm of your hand. The butterfly goes on searching for a passionflower vine. Only on the spiraling tendrils of this vine will she lay her yellow eggs.

vanilla bean

orchid bee

vanilla orchid

pygmy marmoset

The passionflower vine twines around a fruiting fig tree. Figs are the favorite snack of a flock of toucans. Each toucan uses the sawlike edge of its bill to snip off figs. It holds the fruit at the tip of its bill and tosses the fig up in the air to catch it . . . *gulp*.

Next to the toucans, a parrot balances on one foot, using the other to pluck figs from the tree. The woolly monkeys use both hands to eat figs while hanging by their tails. Each of these creatures helps spread the fig tree seeds by dropping many of them as they eat.

fig branch

South American
blue & gold macaw

woolly monkey

passionflower

Without warning, a fruit falls from a cannonball tree. The fruit is so big and heavy that it crashes through the leaves, startling the fig eaters. With a burst of colors, the parrots and toucans take flight.

The woolly monkeys swing into a tree with leaves like umbrellas. On a branch below them, three sharp hooks mean they have company.

toco toucan

scarlet macaw

cannonball tree fruit

rainbow or keel-billed toucan

Those sharp hooks are the claws of a three-toed sloth. It is hanging upside-down from a cecropia tree branch.

The sloth does everything upside-down, even sleep. Its shaggy fur is parted on its belly and hangs down so that rain rolls off. The sloth moves no faster than four feet per minute, making it the slowest mammal of all. It is so slow that greenish algae grows on its fur.

The greenish color helps it blend in with the leaves so that a passing jaguar does not even see it.

liana blossom

jaguar

tropical orchid

three-toed
sloth and baby

The sloth lifts its arm like a slow-motion dancer and begins its weekly journey to the floor of the forest. Lowering itself through the leafy canopy, down into the bushy understory, it will pass by white-faced capuchin monkeys and two other neighbors who have grasping tails.

The kinkajou is sleeping now, but it will wake up at sundown to play and eat. The tamandua is hunting for ants and termites. It tears open an ant nest with its sharp claws and whips out its long, thin, sticky tongue to eat the ants. These and many other creatures live in the trees. Some never visit the ground far below.

white-faced
capuchin

kinkajou

tamandua &
termite nest

There are many plants that live in the trees too with their roots in the air and not in the dirt.

The bromeliad, like a pineapple, has long spikey leaves which circle round and round and form a cone in the middle. Inside this cone is a very small pond, filled with rain water. Salamanders come here to lay eggs. Tree frogs bring their tadpoles here to grow up. Many snails and beetles live their entire lives in this bromeliad pond.

salamander

bromeliad

tree frog tadpole
(poison arrow frog)

stink bug

A bright green anole lizard on its way down the tree stops for a sip of water at a bromeliad pond.

A lot of activity goes on nearby. Bees search for fresh pollen. Harlequin beetles eat nourishing tree sap. A ruby topaz hummingbird seems suspended in midair though it is beating its wings fifty times each second. It hovers while drinking nectar from the flowers of the vines.

A scampering squirrel monkey scurries right through onto the next tree, knocking a ripe cacao pod full of chocolatey seeds to the ground — *kerplunk.*

cocoa pod

harlequin beetle

ruby topaz hummingbird

anole lizard

On the dim forest floor, rests a leaf butterfly that looks just like a fallen leaf. Next to it, a giant walking stick is disguised as a twig. It watches millipedes, spiders, and ants on their daily search for food.

Some leaf cutter ants have just come out of their nest and are climbing one by one up a tree. They will chew off pieces of leaves and bring them back to their nest. Other leaf cutter ants are already returning to the nest with leaves to chew into wet mush. They use the mush to grow a mushroom-like fungus for their food.

leaf cutter worker ants

leaf butterfly

millipede

giant walking stick

What seemed to be a long, slender vine when the ants passed by is an emerald boa, a tree snake, who is watching for its next bite to eat.

It slithers across the trunk of a rubber tree. Slashes in the bark show that a person has been there gathering sap to make into latex rubber.

The emerald boa tries to sneak up on an iguana. Even though the iguana knows there is danger, it doesn't move until the snake is ready to strike. Then the iguana easily escapes by dropping into a stream below.

bignone liana

emerald tree boa

common iguana

monstera or swiss cheese plant

From the stream, the iguana sees brilliant blue morpho butterflies passing by a tapir who usually sleeps all day but has awakened to get a drink of water.

The iguana traces the source of a "tweetle tweet" sound to the other edge of the stream. There a capybara grazes like a gigantic guinea pig. It peacefully munches the long grasses and moist water lilies.

The iguana is an excellent underwater swimmer so it dives below to swim back to the riverbank.

Below the surface, however, the waters are becoming murky.

Amazonian
katydid

capybara

Brazilian tapir
and baby

queen's wreath

Before people began chopping down the trees, the waters of the stream were deep and crystal clear. Now, when it rains, there are fewer tree roots to hold the earth and soak up the water. The red mud slides into the river instead of being held together by tree roots.

If the trees continue to be cut down, the creatures and plants you saw in this book will disappear. Many others will disappear, too. Over half of the creatures in the world make their homes in tropical rain forests. There are so many different kinds of plants and animals that we don't even know them all yet.

People are learning how each kind of plant and animal is needed to keep the rain forest healthy. And, most importantly, we are learning that only people can save the rain forests.

emergent layer

upper canopy

lower canopy

bushy understory

ground layer